Quick Changeover for Operators

The SMED System

SHOPFLOOR SERIES

Quick Changeover for Operators

The SMED System

Created by
The Productivity Press
Development Team

Based on
A Revolution in Manufacturing:
The SMED System
by Shigeo Shingo

PRODUCTIVITY
productivity press

Productivity Press • New York

Most Productivity Press books are available at quantity discounts when purchased in bulk. For more information contact our Customer Service Department (800-394-6868). Address all other inquiries to:

Productivity Press
444 Park Avenue South, Suite 604
New York, NY 10016
United States of America
Telephone: 212-686-5900
Telefax: 212-686-5411
E-mail: info@productivityinc.com

Instructional design and development by Liz MacDonell, Write One Consulting, Portland, Oregon
Book and cover design by William Stanton
Cover illustration by Gary Ragaglia, The Vision Group
Interior illustrations by Matthew C. DeMaio
Additional design and composition by Matthew C. DeMaio, and by William H. Brunson
    Typography Services
Printed and bound by Malloy Lithographing, Inc. in the United States of America

Library of Congress Cataloging-in-Publication Data

Quick changeover for operators : the SMED system / created by the Productivity Press Development
    Team : with a publisher's message by Norman Bodek.
        p.   cm.
    Based on: A revolution in manufacturing / Shigeo Shingo.
    Includes bibliographical references.
    ISBN 1-56327-125-7 (paperback)
    1. Assembly-line methods. 2. Machine-tools. 3. Manufacturing processes.
I. Shingō, Shigeo, 1909–1990. Shinguru dandori e no gententeki shikō. II. Productivity Press
Development Team.
TS178.4.Q53 1996
670.42'7—dc20   96-17512
                                                                                       CIP

06 05   15 14 13 12 11 10

Contents

Chapter 3. Getting Ready for SMED

Chapter 4. Stage 1: Separating Internal and External Setup

Chapter 5. Stage 2: Converting Internal Setup to External Setup

Chapter 6. Stage 3: Streamlining All Aspects of the Setup Operation

Chapter 7. Reflections and Conclusions

About the Authors

Publisher's Message

The book you are holding is intended to give you powerful knowledge that you can use to make your workplace more productive, and your job simpler and more satisfying. It's about how to do equipment or product changeovers in record time—often in under 10 minutes. The method you will learn about here is called SMED, which is short for "Single-Minute Exchange of Die" (the "single" here means a single-digit number of minutes—less than 10).

In one of the first applications of the SMED approach, Toyota shortened setup on a 1,000-ton stamping press from 4 hours to 3 minutes. Quick changeovers are critical for any company that wants to do just-in-time or one-piece flow manufacturing, since they make it possible to switch models easily and avoid making unneeded inventory. The SMED system you will learn about here is the most effective approach for shortening changeover time. SMED will reduce difficult, time-consuming, and wasteful activities in your company, which should support the company's competitiveness and make your own work easier.

The SMED approach is simple and universal. It works in companies all over the world. Although it was first used in (and named for) manufacturing with dies, the basic principles of SMED have been used to reduce setup and turnaround time in all types of manufacturing, assembly, and even service industries, from process and packaging plants to airlines.

SMED is really about thinking about changeover in a new way. Shigeo Shingo, the developer of SMED, learned a great deal by observing what people actually did during changeover and thinking carefully about how the necessary setup work could be done with the shortest possible downtime. Shingo often taught SMED by telling stories about changeover improvements. It was easy to relate to the managers and employees he told about—like most people, they were used to doing things in a certain way. And you could imagine the cartoon light bulb going on when the people in the story realized there was a better way to do the job. We hope this book captures some of the flavor of Shingo's thinking.

Quick Changeover for Operators was developed from a longer book, *A Revolution in Manufacturing: The SMED System*, which was written for managers. When you get right down to it, though, you—the frontline production and assembly associates—are the people who will be most involved in implementing the SMED approach—and also the ones who will benefit the most from it. We have developed this book specifically to give you the basics of SMED in a straightforward and interesting format. Once you understand these basics, you can see how they might apply to your specific situation at work.

This book presents an overview of the reasons why SMED is important for companies and employees, sets out the three basic stages of SMED, and then devotes a separate chapter to each of these stages. The first chapter of the book is like an "owner's manual" that tells you how to get the most out of your reading by using margin assists, summaries, and other features of the book to help you pull out what you need to know.

One of the most effective ways to use this book is to read and discuss it with other employees in group learning sessions. We have deliberately planned the book so that it can be used this way, with chunks of information that can be covered in a series of short sessions. (Most chapters can be covered in a single session; Chapters 5 and 6 contain a lot of examples, and each should probably be covered in two sessions.) Each chapter includes reflection questions to stimulate group discussion. A Learning Package is also available, which includes a leader's guide, overhead transparencies to summarize major points, and color slides showing examples of SMED applications in different kinds of companies.

We hope this book and Learning Package will tell you what you need to know to be involved in a SMED implementation and show you how SMED can make your workplace a better place to spend your time.

Acknowledgments

We at Productivity deeply appreciate the life work of the late Shigeo Shingo, developer of the SMED system and author of *A Revolution in Manufacturing: The SMED System*, the book upon which *Quick Changeover for Operators* is based. Dr. Shingo's years of observation and thinking about changeover have changed the face of manufacturing around the world. We are grateful for the opportunity to share this powerful technique with a wider audience.

This book is modeled after the instructional design developed for 5S *for Operators* (Productivity Press, 1996) by Melanie Rubin of Productivity, Inc. Many people contributed to the design, editing, and content of that pioneering Shopfloor Series book. In particular, Dee Tadlock of Read Right Systems gave extensive instructional design input and review to this series. Productivity, Inc. product developer Tom Fabrizio also contributed instructional design input and advice. The form and content of the Shopfloor Series books were heavily influenced by feedback from Productivity customers, including participants in two focus groups and readers who reviewed the manuscript. Mary Pat Crum, Tim Hickey, Carla Comarella and Patricia Slote of the Productivity Press sales and marketing team also provided input to the overall product concept and design.

Special thanks to Todd Morton, Bryan Kelley, and Jody Maxson of Continental Mills, Inc., for their assistance with changeover examples and the operation checklist in Chapter 4.

Within Productivity Press, the development of *Quick Changeover for Operators* has been a strong team effort. Steven Ott and Diane Asay played major roles in the product definition, development, and editorial stages. Karen Jones served as project manager, with outline, text extraction and development, and illustration concepts by instructional designer Liz MacDonell of Write One Consulting, and with design, production of illustrations and cartoons, and page composition by Matthew C. DeMaio, and final layout and typography by William H. Brunson Typography Services. Art director Bill Stanton created the book and cover design, with cover illustration by Gary Ragaglia of The Vision Group. Susan Swanson managed the prepress production and manufacturing, with editorial and proofreading assistance from Julie Zinkus and Pauline Sullivan.

Finally, the staff at Productivity Press wishes to acknowledge the good work of the many people who are now in the process of implementing the SMED system in their own organizations. We welcome any feedback about this book, as well as input about how we can continue to serve you in your SMED implementation efforts.

SMED's Conceptual Stages

Preliminary
Internal and external setup not differentiated

1
Separate internal and external setup

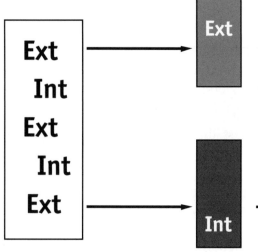

1. Checklists
2. Function checks
3. Improved transport of parts and tools

and Practical Techniques

2	3
Convert internal setup to external setup	Streamline all aspects of setup operations

Ext

1. Advance preparation of operating conditions
2. Function standardization
3. Intermediary jigs

Int

Ext

1. Improved storage and management of of parts and tools

Int

1. Parallel operations
2. Functional clamps
3. Eliminating adjustments
4. Mechanization

Chapter 1
Getting Started

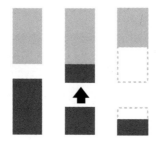

Purpose of This Book

Key Point

Quick Changeover for Operators was written to give you the information you need to participate in implementing the *SMED* system in your workplace. SMED is short for *Single-Minute Exchange of Die*. The goal of SMED is to dramatically shorten changeover times.

What This Book Is Based On

BACKGROUND INFO

Quick Changeover for Operators is based on Shigeo Shingo's book called *A Revolution in Manufacturing: The SMED System*, also published by Productivity Press (see Figure 1-1).

It took Mr. Shingo 19 years to develop SMED. As he studied the setup operations of many factories, he discovered two important facts that are the basis of SMED:

1. Setup operations can be divided into two categories:

    • **Internal setup:** operations that must be performed while the machine is stopped.

    • **External setup:** operations that can be performed while the machine is still running.

2. By shifting as many internal setup operations as possible to external setup operations, changeover times can be drastically reduced, while machines can remain in operation longer.

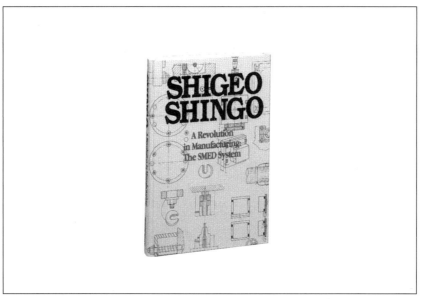

Figure 1-1. *A Revolution in Manufacturing: The SMED System,* by Shigeo Shingo

The book you are currently reading presents the main concepts and tools of Mr. Shingo's book in a shortened and simplified version that requires less time and effort to read than the original book.

The original book is useful as a reference for more detailed information, including case studies on implementing a SMED system in various kinds of workplaces.

Two Ways to Use This Book

There are at least two ways to use this book:

1. As the reading material for a learning group or study group process within your company.

2. For learning on your own.

Productivity Press offers a Learning Package that uses *Quick Changeover for Operators* as the foundation reading material for a learning group. Your company may decide instead to design its own learning group process based on *Quick Changeover for Operators.* Or, you may read this book for individual learning without formal group discussion.

How to Get the Most Out of Your Reading

Becoming Familiar with This Book as a Whole

There are a few steps you can follow to make it easier to absorb the information in this book. We've included a suggested amount of time for each step, but take as much time as you need to become familiar with the material.

How-to Steps

1. Scan the Table of Contents to see how *Quick Changeover for Operators* is set up. (1 minute)

2. Read the rest of this chapter for an overview of the book's contents. (5 minutes)

3. Flip through the book to get a feel for its style, flow, and design. Notice how the chapters are structured and glance at the pictures. (5 minutes)

4. Read parts of Chapter 7, "Reflections and Conclusions," to get a sense for the book's direction. (2 minutes)

Becoming Familiar with Each Chapter

For each chapter in *Quick Changeover for Operators* we suggest you follow these steps to get the most out of your reading:

How-to Steps

1. Read the "Chapter Overview" on the first page to get a feel for the path the chapter follows. (1 minute)

2. Flip through the chapter, looking at the way it is laid out. (1 minute)

3. Ask yourself, Based on what I've seen in this chapter so far, what questions do I have about the material? (3 minutes)

4. Now read the chapter. How long this takes depends on what you already know about the content, and what you are trying to get out of your reading. Enhance your reading by doing the following:

   • Use the margin assists to help you follow the flow of information.

   • If the book is your own, use a highlighter to mark key information and answers to your questions about the material. If the book is not your own, take notes on a separate piece of paper.

   • Answer the "Take Five" questions in the text. These will help you absorb the information by reflecting on how you can implement it.

5. Read the "Chapter Summary" to confirm what you have learned. If you don't remember something in the summary, find that section in the chapter and review it. (5 minutes)

6. Finally, read the "Reflections" questions at the end of the chapter. Think about these questions and write down your answers. (5 minutes)

TAKE FIVE

Take five minutes to think about these questions and to write down your answers:

- What is the overall purpose of this book?

- How might you become familiar with the structure of the book and of each chapter?

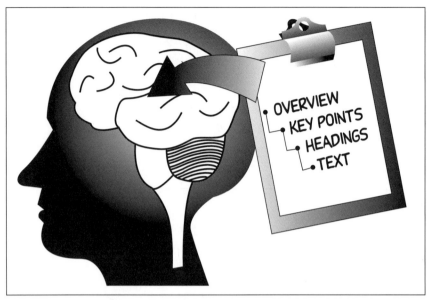

Figure 1-2. Giving Your Brain a Framework for Learning

Explanation of Reading Strategy

Key Point

Reading strategy is based on two simple points about the way people learn. The first point is this: *It's difficult for your brain to absorb new information if it does not have a structure to place it in.* As an analogy, imagine trying to build a house without putting a framework in place first.

Like building a frame for a house, you can give your brain a framework for the new information in the book by getting an overview of the contents and then flipping through the materials. Within each chapter, you repeat this process on a smaller scale by reading the overview, key points, and headings before reading the text (see Figure 1-2).

Key Point

The second point about learning is this: *It is a lot easier to learn if you take in the information one layer at a time, instead of trying to absorb it all at once.* It's like finishing the walls of a house: First you lay down a coat of primer. When it's dry, you apply a coat of paint, and later a final finish coat.

When reading a book, many people think they should start with the first word and read straight through until the end. This is not usually the best way to learn from a book. The method we've described on pages 4 and 5 is easier, more fun, and more effective.

Using the Margin Assists

As you've noticed by now, this book uses small images called *margin assists* to help you follow the information in each chapter. There are five types of margin assists:

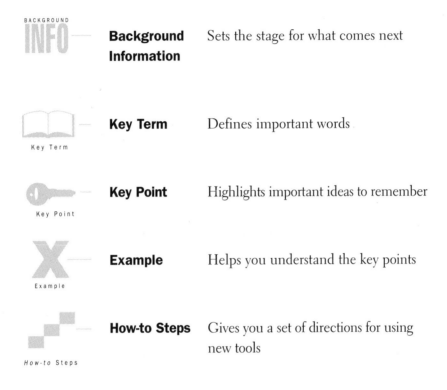

Background Information Sets the stage for what comes next

Key Term Defines important words

Key Point Highlights important ideas to remember

Example Helps you understand the key points

How-to Steps Gives you a set of directions for using new tools

TAKE FIVE

Take five minutes to think about these questions and to write down your answers:

• How can you help yourself learn more from this book (and other reading material in the future)?

• What are margin assists? How do you expect they will help you follow the information in the book?

Overview of the Contents

Chapter 1. Getting Started (pages 1-11)

This is the chapter you're reading now. It explains the purpose of *Quick Changeover for Operators* and how it was written. Then it gives tips for getting the most out of your reading. Finally, it gives you an overview of each chapter.

Chapter 2. Important Terms and Concepts (pages 13-21)

Chapter 2 introduces and defines *Single-Minute Exchange of Die* (SMED). It also explains why SMED is important for companies and how SMED will benefit you. Next, it introduces and defines several important terms and concepts which will help you understand the rest of the book.

Chapter 3. Getting Ready for SMED (pages 23-29)

Chapter 3 explains the four basic steps in a traditional setup procedure. It then begins to prepare you for moving toward SMED by describing the procedure for analyzing your current setup operations. Finally, it introduces you to the three stages of SMED.

Chapter 4. Stage 1: Separating Internal and External Setup (pages 31-39)

Chapter 4 introduces and defines the first stage of SMED, *Separating Internal and External Setup*. It describes and provides examples of three practical techniques that help us separate setup operations: checklists, function checks, and improved transport of dies and other parts.

Chapter 5. Stage 2: Converting Internal Setup to External Setup (pages 41-51)

Chapter 5 introduces and defines the second stage of SMED, *Converting Internal Setup to External Setup*. It describes and provides examples of three techniques for converting internal setup to external: advance preparation of operating conditions, function standardization, and intermediary jigs.

Chapter 6. Stage 3: Streamlining All Aspects of the Setup Operation (pages 53-70)

Chapter 6 introduces and defines the third stage of SMED, *Streamlining All Aspects of the Setup Operation.* It describes and provides examples of five techniques for making external and internal setups more efficient: streamlining the storage and transport of parts and tools, implementing parallel operations, using functional clamps, eliminating adjustments, and mechanization.

Chapter 7. Reflections and Conclusions (pages 71-75)

Chapter 7 presents reflections on and conclusions to this book. It discusses possibilities for applying what you've learned, and suggests ways for you to create a personal action plan for implementing SMED. Finally, it describes opportunities for further learning about SMED.

In Conclusion

SUMMARY

Quick Changeover for Operators is based on Shigeo Shingo's book, *A Revolution in Manufacturing: The SMED System.* You can read *Quick Changeover* on your own or as part of a study group process within your company.

To get the most out of reading this book, it is important to begin by familiarizing yourself with its contents, structure, and design. Then you can follow specific steps for reading each chapter, which will make your reading more efficient, effective, and enjoyable.

This strategy is based on two principles about the way your brain learns:

1. It is difficult for your brain to absorb new information if it does not have a structure to place it in.

2. It is a lot easier to learn if you take in the information one layer at a time instead of trying to absorb it all at once.

Chapter 1, "Getting Started," is the chapter you have just read. Chapter 2 introduces SMED, its benefits to your company and you, and several terms and concepts that will help you understand SMED. Chapter 3 explains the basic steps in the traditional setup procedure, describes the procedure for analyzing your current setup operation, and introduces the three stages of SMED. Chapters 4 through 6 explain the concepts and tools of implementing each stage of SMED. Chapter 7 presents the conclusions to this book and suggests ways for you to create a SMED system in your workplace.

REFLECTIONS

Now that you have completed this chapter, take five minutes to think about these questions and to write down your answers:

- What did you learn from reading this chapter that stands out as particularly useful or interesting?

- Do you have any questions about the topics presented in this chapter? If so, what are they?

- What information do you still need to fully understand the ideas presented in this chapter?

- How can you get this information?

Chapter 2

Important Terms and Concepts

Introduction: What Is SMED?

SMED stands for *Single-Minute Exchange of Die*. The SMED system is a theory and set of techniques that make it possible to perform equipment setup and changeover operations in under 10 minutes—in other words, in the single-minute range. SMED was originally developed to improve die press and machine tool setups, but its principles apply to changeovers in all types of processes.

It is important to point out that *it may not be possible to reach the single-minute range for all setups, but SMED does dramatically reduce setup times in almost every case.* Shorter setup times, in turn, lead to many benefits for you and for your company.

In the following chapters you will learn what SMED is all about and how it differs from traditional setup operations. You will also learn why it is important and how it can help your workplace be more efficient—and therefore more enjoyable.

Figure 2-1. The Trouble with Large-Lot Production

Why SMED Is Important for Companies

Customers today want a variety of products in just the quantities they need. They expect high quality, a good price, and speedy delivery. SMED helps companies meet these customer needs with less waste by making it cost-effective to produce things in smaller quantities, or *lots*.

Key Term

BACKGROUND

The Trouble with Large-Lot Production

Many companies produce goods in large lots simply because long changeover times make it too costly to change products frequently. As you can see in Figure 2-1, large-lot production has several disadvantages:

- **Inventory waste:** Storing what is not sold costs money and ties up company resources without adding any value to the product.

- **Delay:** Customers must wait for the company to produce entire lots rather than just the quantities a customer needs.

- **Declining quality:** Storing unsold inventory increases the chance that it will have to be scrapped or reworked, which adds cost to the product.

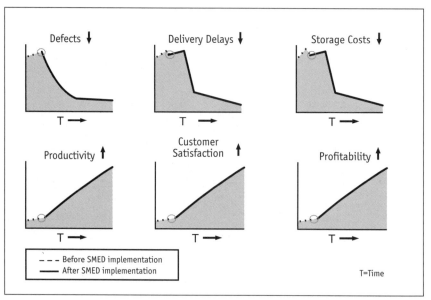

Figure 2-2. Benefits of Shortening Changeover Time with SMED

The Benefits of SMED for Companies

Key Point

SMED changes the assumption that setups have to take a long time. When setups can be done quickly, they can be done as often as needed. This means companies can make products in smaller lots, which has many advantages:

- **Flexibility:** Companies can meet changing customer needs without the expense of excess inventory.

- **Quicker delivery:** Small-lot production means less lead time and less customer waiting time.

- **Better quality:** Less inventory storage means fewer storage-related defects. SMED also lowers defects by reducing setup errors and eliminating trial runs of the new product.

- **Higher productivity:** Shorter changeovers reduce downtime, which means a higher equipment productivity rate.

The benefits of SMED are illustrated in Figure 2-2.

Figure 2-3. SMED Makes Daily Production Go Smoother

The Benefits of SMED for You

Quicker setups also benefit you, the company employees. First, quicker setups support job security by strengthening the company's competitiveness. In addition, as shown in Figure 2-3, quick changeovers as a result of SMED make daily production work go smoother because:

Key Point

- Simpler setups result in safer changeovers, with less physical strain or risk of injury.

- Less inventory means less clutter in the workplace, which makes production itself easier and safer.

- Setup tools are standardized and combined, which means fewer tools to keep track of.

TAKE FIVE

Take five minutes to think about these questions and to write down your answers:

- Based on what you know so far about SMED, can you see how it might benefit your company? If so, how?

- Can you see how SMED might benefit you? If so, how?

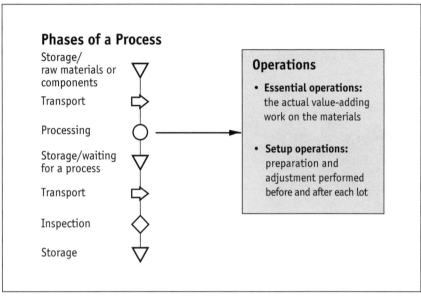

Figure 2-4. How Operations Relate to Processes

Definitions of Important Terms and Concepts

Before we begin talking in detail about the SMED system in the next chapter, it is important to define a few key terms and concepts.

Manufacturing Processes

Key Term

In manufacturing, a *process* is a continuous flow in which raw materials are converted into finished products. In simpler terms, a process is the way something gets made. Manufacturing processes have four basic phases:

1. **Processing**: assembly, disassembly, alteration of shape or quality

2. **Inspection**: comparison with a standard

3. **Transport**: change of location

4. **Storage**: a period of time during which no work, transportation, or inspection is performed on the product

Materials often go through several of these phases throughout the manufacturing process. The left side of Figure 2-4 shows a typical sequence of process phases.

Manufacturing Operations

Key Term

An *operation*, by contrast, is any action performed by workers or machines on the raw materials, work-in-process, or finished products. It's what you do to make something.

Key Point

Manufacturing production is a network of operations and processes. Referring back to Figure 2-4, each phase of the manufacturing process has one or more corresponding operations. These operations include setup operations as well as essential operations such as the actual machining of material. In this book we will focus on setup operations related to the processing phase.

Setup Operations

Key Term

A *setup operation* (or simply *setup*) is the preparation or after-adjustment that is performed once before and once after each lot is processed.

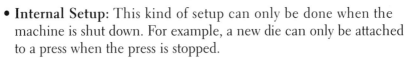

Key Term

There are two kinds of setup operations:

- **Internal Setup:** This kind of setup can only be done when the machine is shut down. For example, a new die can only be attached to a press when the press is stopped.
- **External Setup:** This kind of setup can be done while the machine is still running. For example, bolts to attach to the die can be assembled and sorted while the press is operating.

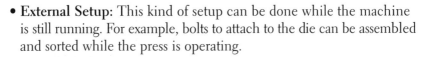

TAKE FIVE

Take five minutes to think about these questions and to write down your answers:

- What kinds of processes and operations do you perform in your daily work?
- Think about your setup process. Which operations are performed while the machine is running? While the machine is stopped?

In Conclusion

SUMMARY

SMED is a theory and set of techniques that make it possible to perform equipment setup and changeover operations in under 10 minutes. While it may not be possible to perform all setups in under 10 minutes with SMED, it does reduce setup times dramatically.

By making setup times quicker and simpler, SMED helps companies produce smaller lots. This means they can meet their customers' needs for high-quality, low-cost products that are delivered quickly and without the expense of excess inventory.

Quicker setups also benefit you. They support job security by strengthening the company's competitiveness. They also make daily production work smoother because simpler setups are safer, the workplace is less cluttered, and there are fewer tools to keep track of.

Manufacturing production is a network of processes and operations. A process is a continuous flow in which raw materials are converted into finished products. Processes have four basic phases: processing, inspection, transportation, and storage.

An operation is any action performed by workers or machines as the product is being made. Each of the four process phases includes setup operations as well as essential operations such as the actual machining of material. In this book we will focus on setup operations related to the processing phase.

A setup is the preparation or after-adjustment that is performed once before and once after each lot is processed. There are two kinds of setup operations: internal setup, which can only be done when the machine is shut down, and external setup, which can be done while the machine is still running.

REFLECTIONS

Now that you have completed this chapter, take five minutes to think about these questions and to write down your answers:

- What did you learn from reading this chapter that stands out as particularly useful or interesting?

- Do you have any questions about the topics presented in this chapter? If so, what are they?

- What information do you still need to fully understand the ideas presented in this chapter?

- How can you get this information?

Chapter 3

Getting Ready for SMED

CHAPTER OVERVIEW

Basic Steps in a Setup Operation

- Preparation, After-Process Adjustments, Checking of Materials and Tools
- Mounting and Removing Blades, Tools, and Parts
- Measurements, Settings, and Calibrations
- Trial Runs and Adjustments

Analyzing Your Setup Operations

The Three Stages of SMED

- Stage 1: Separating Internal and External Setup
- Stage 2: Converting Internal Setup to External Setup
- Stage 3: Streamlining All Aspects of the Setup Operation

In Conclusion

- Summary
- Reflections

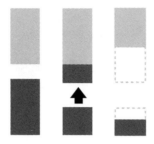

Basic Steps in a Setup Operation

Key Point

In the previous chapter you learned that internal and external setup operations are included in each of the four manufacturing process phases. *Similarly, all setup operations that have not been improved through SMED are made up of four steps—regardless of the type of equipment or operation.* These four steps are:

1. Preparation, after-process adjustments, checking of materials and tools

2. Mounting and removing blades, tools, and parts

3. Measurements, settings, and calibrations

4. Trial runs and adjustments

Key Term

In a *traditional setup*—one in which SMED has not yet been implemented—these steps take the portion of total setup time you see in Figure 3-1. Let's take a closer look at each step.

Preparation, After-Process Adjustments, Checking of Materials and Tools

Key Point

This step ensures that all parts and tools are where they should be and that they are functioning properly. Also included in this step is the period after processing when these items are removed and returned to storage, machinery is cleaned, and so forth.

In a traditional setup, parts of the preparation step are done after the machine is stopped. As we will see in the next chapter, this step should be done as external setup—while the equipment is still running.

Steps in Setup	Proportion of Setup Time Before SMED Improvements
Preparation, After-Process Adjustments, Checking of Materials and Tools	30%
Mounting and Removing Blades, Tools, and Parts	5%
Measurements, Settings, and Calibrations	15%
Trial Runs and Adjustments	50%

Figure 3-1. Basic Setup Steps and Their Time Breakdown Before SMED Improvements

Mounting and Removing Blades, Tools, and Parts

Key Point

This step includes the removal of parts and tools after one lot is processed, and the attachment of the parts and tools for the next lot.

Generally the machine must be stopped to do this step, so it is internal setup. Notice in Figure 3-1 that this internal setup step—the actual changing over—takes very little time compared to the other steps.

Measurements, Settings, and Calibrations

Key Point

This step refers to all the measurements and calibrations that must be made in order to perform a production operation, such as centering, dimensioning, measuring temperature or pressure, and so forth.

Although the equipment must often be stopped for this step, the SMED system teaches ways to do these tasks quickly by preparing while the equipment is still running.

Trial Runs and Adjustments

Key Point

In the final steps of a traditional setup operation, adjustments are made after a test piece is machined. The more accurate your measurements and calibrations are in the previous step, the easier these adjustments will be.

BACKGROUND

Correct adjustment of the equipment is one of the most difficult tasks in a setup operation. In a traditional setup, the time needed for trial runs and adjustments depends on personal skill. Look back at Figure 3-1 and notice that this step accounts for about half of the time in a traditional setup.

In a traditional setup the machine is not making good products until this step is finished, so it is considered part of internal setup. *SMED teaches ways to eliminate this step completely, so that the machine makes good products right after it is started up.*

Key Point

TAKE FIVE

Take five minutes to think about these questions and to write down your answers:

- About how long does each of the four setup steps take in your operation?

- Which of these steps takes the most time or is the most difficult to get right?

Figure 3-2. Using Videotape to Do a Setup Analysis

Analyzing Your Setup Operations

The main reason traditional setup operations take so long is that internal and external setup are confused. Many tasks that could be done while the machine is still running aren't done until the machine is stopped.

The three stages of SMED described in this book are designed to simplify and shorten changeovers. But before you start applying SMED, you need a clear idea of how you currently perform setup operations and how long each step takes.

Key Term

This preliminary step, called a *setup analysis*, will help you plan how to implement SMED improvements on your equipment. Setup analysis has three main steps:

How-to Steps

1. Videotape the entire setup operation (Figure 3-2), focusing on the hand, eye, and body movements of the person doing the setup. Use the camera's time and date function if there is one.

2. Show the video to the setup person and other people involved with the equipment. Ask the setup person to describe what he or she is shown doing. Have the group share their thoughts about the operation.

3. Study the video in detail, noting the time and motions involved in each step of the setup. Use the video player's pause and rewind functions as needed. Also use a stopwatch if necessary.

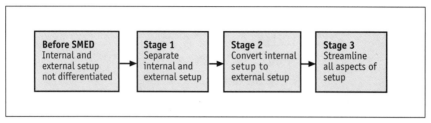

Figure 3-3. The Three Stages of SMED Implementation

The Three Stages of SMED

Key Point

As illustrated in Figure 3-3, *the SMED approach to changeover improvement is implemented in three stages.* Each of these stages will be discussed in detail in Chapters 4, 5, and 6. Let's look at each briefly.

Stage 1: Separating Internal and External Setup

The most important step in implementing SMED is distinguishing between internal and external setup. By doing obvious things like preparation and transport while the machine is running, the time needed for internal setup, with the machine stopped, can usually be cut by as much as 30 to 50 percent.

Stage 2: Converting Internal Setup to External Setup

Further reducing setup times toward the single-minute range involves two important activities: 1) reexamining operations to see whether any steps are wrongly assumed to be internal setup, and 2) finding ways to convert these steps to external setup. Operations can often be converted to external setup by looking at their true function.

Stage 3: Streamlining All Aspects of the Setup Operation

To further reduce setup time, the basic elements of each setup are analyzed in detail. Specific principles are applied to shorten the time needed, especially for steps that must be done as internal setup, with the machine stopped. The figure on pages xii and xiii gives a visual picture of how SMED shortens changeover time (we have placed this in the front part of the book for easy reference.)

In Conclusion

SUMMARY

Setup procedures, regardless of the type of equipment or operation, are made up of four steps. The first step is preparation, after-process adjustments, and checking of materials and tools. The second step is mounting and removing blades, tools, and parts. Next come measurements, settings, and calibrations. The fourth step is trial runs and adjustments.

To get ready for implementing SMED, you must first look at how you currently perform setup operations. This preliminary step is called setup analysis. The three steps in setup analysis are: videotaping the entire setup operation, asking the setup person and others involved with the equipment to talk about what they did, and studying the time and motions involved in each step of the setup.

SMED is implemented in three stages. Stage 1 involves distinguishing between internal and external setup. This step alone can reduce setup time by as much as 30 to 50 percent. Stage 2 involves converting internal setup to external setup. Stage 3 involves streamlining all aspects of the setup operation.

REFLECTIONS

Now that you have completed this chapter, take five minutes to think about these questions and to write down your answers:

- What did you learn from reading this chapter that stands out as particularly useful or interesting?

- Do you have any questions about the topics presented in this chapter? If so, what are they?

- What information do you still need to fully understand the ideas presented in this chapter?

- How can you get this information?

Chapter 4

Stage 1: Separating Internal and External Setup

CHAPTER OVERVIEW

Description of Stage 1

Checklists

Function Checks

Improved Transport of Parts and Tools

- SMED at Work: Die Transport as External Setup

In Conclusion

- Summary
- Reflections

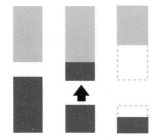

Description of Stage 1

Recall from Chapter 3 that in Stage 1 of SMED, tasks that can be carried out while the machine is operating are separated from tasks that must be performed while the machine is stopped.

Certain tasks can clearly be done before machines are stopped for changeover. These include lining up the right people, preparing parts and tools, making repairs, and bringing the parts and tools closer to the equipment.

In practice, however, it is surprising how often these tasks are done after the machine has been stopped instead of while it is still running the previous lot. Separating these tasks and performing them as external setup can cut changeover time by as much as 30 to 50 percent.

Three practical techniques help us separate internal and external setup tasks. These techniques are: using checklists, performing function checks, and improving transport of dies and other parts. Let's take a look at each of these techniques.

Checklists

Key Term

A *checklist* lists everything required to set up and run the next operation. The list includes such items as:

- Tools, specifications, and workers required
- Proper values for operating conditions such as temperature, pressure, current, and feed rate
- Correct measurements and dimensions required for each operation

Operation Checklist effective 4/30			
Equipment: Line C Casepacker **Operation:** Changeover to 3.5 lb size **Date:** 5/7			
	Employees trained for setup and operation (need 2 people)		
	Colleen R.	✔	Jody M.
✔	Elizabeth B.		Kyle B.
	Tools needed		
✔	automatic nut driver		
✔	hex wrench		
	rolling cart —at Line B 'til 10:30		
	Parts needed		
✔	elevator plate—3.5 lb. size		
✔	compression plate—3.5 lb. size		
✔	feed augur—3.5 lb. size		
✔	vacuum hose, towels, brushes for cleandown		
	Standard Operating Procedures to follow		
✔	SOP 001 (changeover)	✔	SOP 003 (cleandown)

Figure 4-1. An Operation Checklist Helps You Prepare for Changeovers

Key Point

A sample checklist is shown in Figure 4-1. *Checking items off the list before the machine is stopped helps prevent oversights and mistakes that otherwise might come up after internal setup has begun.* Using a checklist also helps you avoid errors and multiple test runs later.

Key Point

It is very important to establish a specific checklist for each machine or operation. Using general checklists for an entire shop can be confusing. General checklists also tend to get lost and are often ignored.

TAKE FIVE

Take five minutes to think about these questions and to write down your answers:

• What tasks and tools would you include in a checklist for your changeover process?

• How would a checklist help you run the operation more smoothly?

Figure 4-2. Function Checks Can Save Time and Trouble

Function Checks

Key Term

A checklist helps you determine that you have all the tools you need for a particular operation. The next step, the *function check*, tells you whether the parts are in perfect working order.

Key Point

Function checks should be done well before setup begins so that repairs can be made if something does not work right. If broken dies, molds, or jigs are not discovered until test runs are done, a delay will occur in internal setup (see Figure 4-2). Making sure such items are in working order *before* they are mounted will cut down setup time a great deal.

TAKE FIVE

Take five minutes to think about these questions and to write down your answers:

• In your setup process, what parts could you perform a function check on during external setup?

• How would you make sure the parts are in working order?

Improved Transport of Parts and Tools

Dies, molds, tools, jigs, gauges, and other items needed for an operation must be moved between storage areas and machines, then back to storage once a lot is finished. *To shorten the time the machine is shut down, transport of these items should be done during external setup.* In other words, new parts and tools should be transported to the machine before the machine is shut down for changeover. Likewise, old parts and other tools should not be put away until the new parts are installed and the machine is started up for the next product.

If the machine is automated, the operator may be able to handle the transport alone; other times, transport of parts and tools may require coordination with another worker who is assigned the task of moving. In either case, improving transport may involve taking a new look at your current procedure from the viewpoint of shortening machine downtime.

The case example on the next two pages illustrates this new way of thinking about die transport.

TAKE FIVE

Take five minutes to think about these questions and to write down your answers:

- In your setup process, what dies or other items could you transport during external setup? How?

- How would this effort save you time?

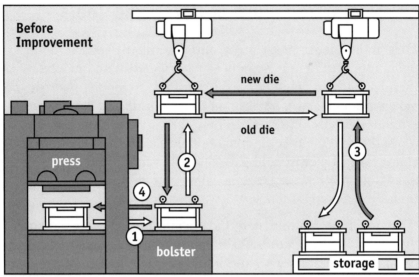

Figure 4-3. Before Improvement: Putting Away the Old Die Before Loading the New One

SMED at Work: Die Transport as External Setup

Procedure Before Improvement

Example

At Y Industries, one production area used the following procedures, illustrated in Figure 4-3, for changing heavy dies on a large press:

1. After the machine was stopped, the old die was extracted from the machine onto a moving bolster.

2. A crane hoisted the old die from the moving bolster, carried it to the storage area, and lowered it.

3. The crane then hoisted the new die from the storage area and transported it to the moving bolster.

4. The new die was mounted and the machine was started up again for production.

This changeover procedure seemed sensible and efficient because it involved just two hoisting operations. However, no one thought about the fact that the machine was not productive during the time it took to put away the old die and carry in the new one.

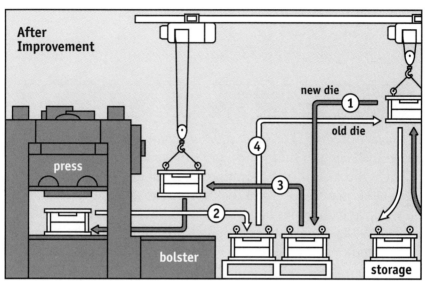

Figure 4-4. After Improvement: Loading the New Die Before Storing the Old One

Procedure After Improvement

After analyzing the transportation involved in the setup, the employees changed their procedure to the following steps, shown in Figure 4-4:

1. Before the machine was shut down, the crane brought the new die and placed it next to the machine.

2. The machine finished the previous operation and was stopped. The old die was removed onto the moving bolster. The crane hoisted the old die from the bolster, then set it down near the machine.

3. Next, the crane hoisted the new die onto the moving bolster. The new die was mounted and the machine was started up.

4. After the machine began the new operation, the crane hoisted the old die and returned it to the storage area.

Key Point

When this sequence was first suggested, the area supervisor was opposed to it. He thought it would be inefficient because it involved several more hoisting operations. *He changed his mind, however, when he realized that they could produce five more units of the new product during the time it took to transport the old die to storage.* The important point here is to shorten the time the machine is shut down.

In Conclusion

SUMMARY

Stage 1 of SMED is *Separation of Internal and External Setup Tasks*. In other words, tasks that can be carried out while the machine is operating are separated from tasks that must be performed while the machine is stopped. Three practical techniques help us separate internal and external setup tasks: checklists, function checks, and improved transport of dies and other parts.

A checklist lists everything required to set up and run the next operation. By using a checklist, you can double-check that all the items, people, and information you need are where they should be. Doing this before you begin an operation helps you avoid errors and multiple test runs later.

A function check tells you whether the parts are in perfect working order. Failure to perform function checks before beginning a changeover can lead to delays in internal setup. A function check enables you to make any needed repairs before the next changeover.

Finally, to cut down on internal setup time, plan to transport the items you need for the changeover during external setup rather than while the machine is stopped. Don't put away the old items until you have started the machine again.

REFLECTIONS

Now that you have completed this chapter, take five minutes to think about these questions and to write down your answers:

- What did you learn from reading this chapter that stands out as particularly useful or interesting?

- Do you have any questions about the topics presented in this chapter? If so, what are they?

- What information do you still need to fully understand the ideas presented in this chapter?

- How can you get this information?

Chapter 5

Stage 2: Converting Internal Setup to External Setup

CHAPTER OVERVIEW

Description of Stage 2

Advance Preparation of Operating Conditions

Function Standardization

- Implementing Function Standardization
- SMED at Work: Standardizing the Clamping Function of Press Dies
- SMED at Work: Using Jigs to Center the Die
- SMED at Work: Using a Die Cassette System

Intermediary Jigs

- SMED at Work: Using Intermediary Jigs for Multiple Press Dies
- SMED at Work: Using Intermediary Jigs in Profile Milling Machines

In Conclusion

- Summary
- Reflections

Description of Stage 2

BACKGROUND
INFO

In Stage 1 of SMED, tasks that can be carried out while the machine is operating are separated from tasks that must be performed while the machine is stopped. But Stage 1 alone cannot reduce internal setup time into the single-minute range. For that, you must implement Stage 2, *Converting Internal Setup to External Setup.*

There are two steps in Stage 2:

How-to Steps

1. Look at the true functions and purposes of each operation in your current internal setup.

2. Find ways to convert these internal setup steps to external setup.

An example of converting internal setup tasks to external setup is preheating die molds that have always been heated only after setup has begun. Another example is shifting centering to an external task by doing it outside the machine on a standardized jig.

Key Point

The key to successful implementation of Stage 2 is allowing yourself to look at your current internal setup as if you are seeing it for the first time. Do not let old habits and beliefs get in the way of making changes.

Three practical techniques help shift internal setup tasks to external setup. These techniques are: preparing operating conditions in advance, standardizing essential functions, and using intermediary jigs. Let's take a look at each of these techniques.

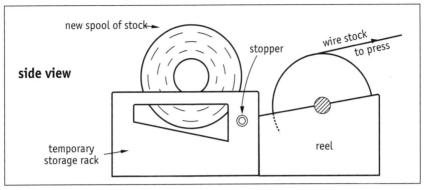

Figure 5-1. Temporary Holder for Wire Stock

Advance Preparation of Operating Conditions

Key Term

Advance preparation of operating conditions means getting necessary parts, tools, and conditions ready before internal setup begins. Conditions like temperature, pressure, or position of materials can often be prepared externally, while the machine is running.

Example

One example involves wire stock supplied on heavy spools. New spools must be brought to the machine by forklift, but a forklift isn't always available right away. To avoid unproductive downtime, a temporary holder such as the one shown in Figure 5-1 can be built. The holder is loaded with a new spool while the machine is still running. When the end of the old roll is reached, the operator simply pushes the new roll into position and continues.

Example

Another example of advance preparation is preheating machine parts or materials outside the machine to the temperature needed for processing. Some companies conserve energy by using heat given off by other equipment for this task.

TAKE FIVE

Take five minutes to think about these questions and to write down your answers:

• What conditions and materials in your process can be prepared in advance of internal setup?

• How would this effort affect your internal setup time?

Function Standardization

When tools or machine parts in a new operation are different from those in the previous one, operators must make time-consuming adjustments during changeover—often with the machine shut down. Standardization—keeping something the same from one operation to another—helps get rid of this internal setup.

SMED uses a targeted approach called *function standardization.* It would be expensive and wasteful to make the external dimensions of every die, tool, or part the same, regardless of the size or shape of the product it forms. Function standardization avoids this waste by focusing on standardizing only those elements whose functions are essential to the setup. Function standardization might apply to dimensioning, centering, securing, expelling, or gripping, for instance.

Implementing Function Standardization

Implementing function standardization involves two steps:

1. Look closely at each individual function in your setup process and decide which functions, if any, can be standardized.

2. Look again at the functions and think about which can be made more efficient by replacing the fewest possible parts.

The quickest way to replace something, of course, is to replace nothing at all—or as little as possible. A simple example of function standardization involves the feed bar on a transfer die press. The feed bar performs three operations: gripping the product, sending the product to the next process, and returning the feed bar to its original position. When changing to a different product, only the gripping function needs to change to match the new shape, dimension, or material. There is no need to replace the entire bar—it is enough to switch the finger section attached to the tip.

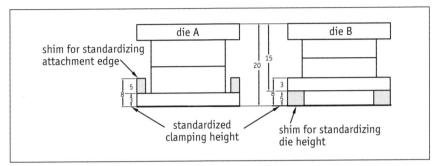

Figure 5-2. Using Shims to Standardize Die Height and Clamping Height

SMED at Work: Standardizing the Clamping Function of Press Dies

Example

In the setup procedure for a press, adjusting the shut height of the die requires a lot of skill. Many people think it can only be done during internal setup, with the machine shut down. Function standardization of the part of the die that must be clamped to the machine can shorten internal setup time dramatically by making shut height adjustment unnecessary.

Suppose you have two dies like the ones shown in Figure 5-2. Die A has a 20-inch shut height and die B has a 15-inch shut height. Without function standardization, operators changing from one die to another would have to make a lot of adjustments on the machine in order to clamp on the new, differently sized die.

Function standardization solves the problem by using simple shim devices to make the shut height and clamping height the same for both dies. Here's how it works:

How-to Steps

1. The difference in height between the two dies is figured out. In this case, the difference is 5 inches.

2. Two shims, each 5 inches in height, are placed under the shorter die (die B). Now die B plus the shims equals the height of die A (20 inches).

3. Notice that the clamping height for die B is 8 inches with the shims in place (3-inch edge plus 5-inch shims). Since the goal is to standardize the clamping height of both dies, add two 5-inch shims on top of die A's attachment edge. Now it also has a clamping height of 8 inches.

Standardizing the clamping height makes it possible to use the same clamping bolts for both dies. This cuts out most of the adjustment work.

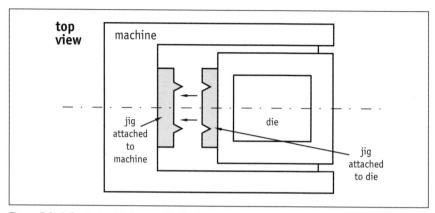

Figure 5-3. A Centering Jig Automatically Positions the Die or Part

SMED at Work: Using Jigs to Center the Die

Example

When setting up a press, the die must be positioned in the center of the bolster. Some small dies have shanks on the top that must fit exactly into the shank attachment hole in the ram of the press. To get the die precisely centered for this, the traditional method was to inch the ram downward while aligning the shank and hole by sight. This was done slowly and cautiously, since the die could be destroyed if the ram was not correctly aligned. The operation was time-consuming and difficult.

The operation can be improved with function standardization as shown in Figure 5-3 (top view). A centering jig is attached to the machine so that the edge of the jig is a fixed distance from the center of the die and shank. This jig has V-shaped projections to the left and right of the center.

Next, a second jig is attached to each die. This jig has two V-shaped notches that match the two projections on the centering jig. The width of this jig is set so that the shaft of the die will be perfectly centered from front to back when the die and jig are pressed against the jig on the machine. And when the V-shaped notches on the die jig interlock with the V-shaped projections on the machine jig, the die will be perfectly centered from left to right.

Using this method, the shank and shank hole match up easily, even when the die is lowered at normal speed. Setting a die to center position becomes an extremely simple operation, which reduces errors and setup time a great deal.

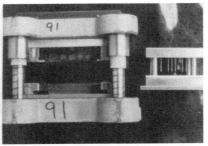

Figure 5-4. Die Cassette System Showing Outer Mechanical Part and Removable Product-Forming Part

SMED at Work: Using a Die Cassette System

Example

A third application of function standardization involves the use of a die cassette system. In this approach, the functions of a die or other part are separated into a mechanical function (applying pressure) and a product-forming function (making a particular change in the shape of the workpiece). To take care of the mechanical function, the mechanical portion of the die is permanently attached to the machine without the product-forming portion.

The product-forming function is then made into a cassette device. Just as an audio cassette can be exchanged according to what music you want to hear, die cassettes can be exchanged according to the function that needs to be performed. In other words, you might have a different cassette for each type of work your process requires and take them in and out of the machine as needed.

In addition to standardizing the mechanical function of the operation, die cassettes are also lighter weight, easier to change over, and require less adjustment. This cassette exchange system is illustrated in Figure 5-4.

TAKE FIVE

Take five minutes to think about this question and to write down your answer:

• How could you apply function standardization to shorten your internal setup?

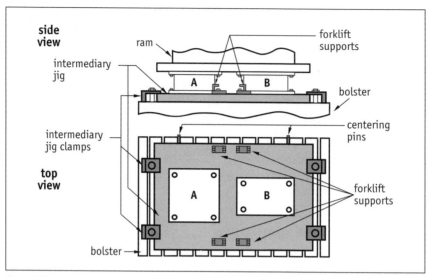

Figure 5-5. Multiple Press Dies Mounted on an Intermediary Jig

Intermediary Jigs

Key Term

In many processes, intermediary jigs can be used to change internal setup tasks into external ones. *Intermediary jigs* are plates or frames of standard dimension that can be removed from the machine.

While the die attached to one of these jigs is being used on the machine, the next die is centered and attached to another jig as an external setup procedure. When the first die is finished, the second jig—with the next die already attached and centered—is mounted on the machine.

Intermediary jigs can also be used to set up workpieces and machine tools. Here are some examples.

SMED at Work: Using Intermediary Jigs for Multiple Press Dies

Example

In the operation illustrated in Figure 5-5, different sets of multiple dies need to be mounted on a large press. Two identical intermediary jig plates are made to hold the dies. While the first jig and dies are in the machine and working, two new dies are attached to the other intermediary jig and centered. When the machine is stopped for changeover, the operator simply exchanges the jigs with the dies attached. This way, internal setup can be completed and the machine started up in just a few short minutes.

Figure 5-6. A Product Template Is Centered on an Intermediary Jig, and the Assembly Is Hoisted into the Milling Machine

SMED at Work: Using Intermediary Jigs in Profile Milling Machines

Example

Form blocks for television picture tubes are machined on a profile milling machine. Centering and setting heights for the template and the workplace are done directly on the machine. This requires a lot of time because of the many curved shapes involved. During this time, the machine is shut down.

Internal setup time can be greatly reduced by using two standardized intermediary jigs. While one item is machined, a template and the next workpiece can be attached to the other intermediary jig (see Figure 5-6, left side). They are then centered and set for the proper height outside the machine.

When the first operation is over, the old jig is removed and the second jig (with the template and attached workpiece) is hoisted into place on the machine (see Figure 5-6, right side). Since the jig is standardized, centering and positioning are now performed easily. And mounting simply requires clamping the jig to a fixed place on the table. As a result, idle time on the milling machine is reduced and productivity increases.

TAKE FIVE

Take five minutes to think about this question and to write down your answer:

• Could intermediary jigs improve internal setup in your operation?

In Conclusion

SUMMARY

Stage 2 of SMED is *Converting Internal Setup to External Setup*. There are two steps: 1) Looking at the true functions and purposes of each operation in your current internal setup, and 2) finding ways to convert these internal setup steps to external setup—things you can do while the machine is still running.

The key to successful implementation of Stage 2 is allowing yourself to look at your current internal setup as if you are seeing it for the first time. Do not allow old habits and beliefs to get in the way of making changes.

Three techniques help shift internal setup tasks to external. Advance preparation of operating conditions involves thinking of ways to get parts, tools, and other items ready before you stop the machine for changeover.

Function standardization means making identical those parts whose functions are essential to the setup. This technique involves two steps: 1) Looking closely at each individual function and deciding which can be standardized, and 2) thinking about which functions can be made more efficient by replacing the fewest parts. The quickest way to replace something, of course, is to replace nothing at all— or as little as possible.

The third technique is using intermediary jigs. In this step, two identical jig plates are prepared and used. While a workpiece or die attached to one of the jigs is processed, the next workpiece or die is centered and attached to another jig. When the first workpiece is finished, it is removed from the machine while still attached to its jig, and the second jig with the next workpiece already positioned on it is mounted on the machine.

REFLECTIONS

Now that you have completed this chapter, take five minutes to think about these questions and to write down your answers:

- What did you learn from reading this chapter that stands out as particularly useful or interesting?

- Do you have any questions about the topics presented in this chapter? If so, what are they?

- What information do you still need to fully understand the ideas presented in this chapter?

- How can you get this information?

Chapter 6

Stage 3: Streamlining All Aspects of the Setup Operation

CHAPTER OVERVIEW

Description of Stage 3

- Streamlining External Setup
- Streamlining Internal Setup

Implementing Parallel Operations

Using Functional Clamps

- One-Turn Methods
- One-Motion Methods
- Interlocking Methods

Eliminating Adjustments

- Fixed Numerical Settings
- Visible Center Lines and Reference Planes
- Least Common Multiple (LCM) System

Mechanization

In Conclusion

- Summary
- Reflections

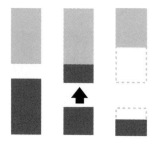

Description of Stage 3

So far we have learned that in Stage 1 of SMED, internal setup tasks are separated from external setup tasks. Then in Stage 2, as many of the remaining internal setup tasks as possible are converted to external setup tasks and done while the equipment is still running.

This brings us to the third and final stage in SMED, *Streamlining All Aspects of the Setup Operation.* In this stage, all of the remaining internal and external setup operations are improved. We do this by looking closely at each operation's function and purpose one more time. Implementing Stage 3 of SMED leads in nearly all cases to setups within the single-minute range.

Practical techniques for Stage 3 improvements can be divided into external setup improvements and internal setup improvements.

Streamlining External Setup

Key Point

External setup improvements include streamlining the storage and transport of parts and tools. In dealing with small tools, dies, jigs, and gauges, it is vital to address issues of tool and die management. You need to ask yourself questions such as:

- What is the best way to organize these items?
- How can we keep these items maintained in perfect condition and ready for the next operation?
- How many of these items should we keep in stock?

An example of one method for streamlining storage and transport is described on the next page.

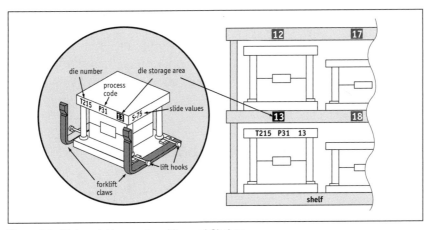

Figure 6-1. "Return Addresses" on Dies and Shelves

SMED at Work: Improving Storage and Transport

Example

Operations for storing and transporting dies can be very time-consuming, especially when your company keeps a large number of dies on hand. Storage and transport can be improved by marking the dies with color codes and the location numbers of the shelves where they are stored, as shown in Figure 6-1. The shelves are also marked with this same "return address" information, making it easy to find dies and return them to their proper storage locations.

In addition, the direction the dies need to face can also be taken into account during reshelving. This way, the next time the die is needed, a lift operator can attach lift hooks to the die without getting off the forklift.

Lastly, die storage and transport can be made much more efficient if the most frequently used dies are stored where they are easiest to retrieve the next time they are needed for an operation.

TAKE FIVE

Take five minutes to think about these questions and to write down your answers:

• What is the best way to organize your small tools and parts?

• Can you think of ways you could improve tools and parts control and storage through color coding or labeling?

Streamlining Internal Setup

Thorough improvements in internal setup operations are next. These include implementing parallel operations, using functional clamps, eliminating adjustments, and mechanization. We'll spend the remainder of this chapter discussing these four approaches.

Implementing Parallel Operations

BACKGROUND INFO

Machines such as large presses, plastic molding machines, and die-casting machines often require operations at both the front and back of the machine. One-person changeovers of such machines mean wasted time and movement because the same person is constantly walking back and forth from one end of the machine to the other. The "Before" side of Figure 6-2 traces the single operator's footsteps.

Key Term

Parallel operations divide the setup operations between two people, one at each end of the machine. With two (or more) people, operations that were once completed in, say, 12 minutes might now take 4, thanks to eliminating the time spent walking back and forth. The "After" side of Figure 6-2 shows the reduced number of steps involved in a parallel operation.

Key Point

Key Term

When setup is done using parallel operations, it is important to maintain reliable and safe operations and minimize waiting time. To help streamline parallel operations, workers develop and follow procedural charts for each setup. A *procedural chart* indicates the sequence of tasks each worker will perform, the time needed for each task, and when safety signals are to be given. Each time one worker has completed an operation, he or she must signal to the other worker—preferably with a buzzer, whistle, or light—to "go ahead" or "wait." By following the procedural chart, everyone involved in the operation knows what to do and when.

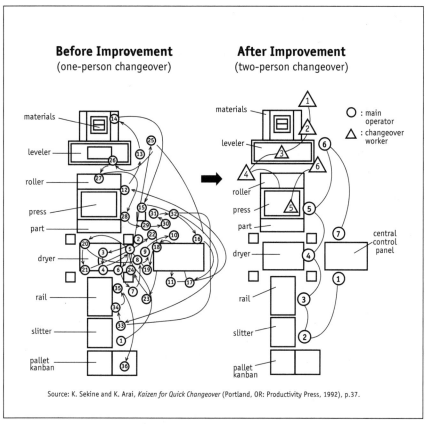

Figure 6-2. Shortening Setups by Using Two People in Parallel Operations

TAKE FIVE

Take five minutes to think about these questions and to write down your answers:

• How would you implement parallel operations on your machine?

• What would the procedural chart for this operation look like?

Using Functional Clamps

In traditional setups, bolts are often used to attach dies or tools directly to the machine. In setups using the SMED system, however, bolts are considered "the enemy." This is because using bolts and nuts as fasteners slows down internal setup in a number of ways. For example:

Key Point

- **Bolts get lost.** Loose bolts and nuts can disappear under machines or roll into floor grates.

- **Bolts get mismatched.** Bolts aren't always standardized, even in one setup. Matching up the right nuts and bolts can take time and searching.

- Most importantly, **bolts take too long to tighten**.

Key Point

People assume that because a nut has 15 threads, the bolt must be turned 15 times to tighten. In reality, those 15 threads are only there to provide the friction that holds the nut, bolt, and die or workpiece in place once the bolt is tightened. *When the purpose of the bolt is simply to fasten or unfasten, turning the bolt another 14 turns is really a waste of time and energy; the releasing and fastening actually happens only on the first and last turns.*

Key Term

To avoid this wasted time and energy, SMED uses devices called functional clamps. A *functional clamp* is an attachment device that holds objects in place with minimal effort. It may use a modified bolt or an entirely different kind of fastener that can be tightened or loosened quickly.

In addition to being much faster, most kinds of functional clamps can stay attached to the machine, so there's nothing to get lost or mismatched.

Functional clamping systems include one-turn, one-motion, and interlocking methods.

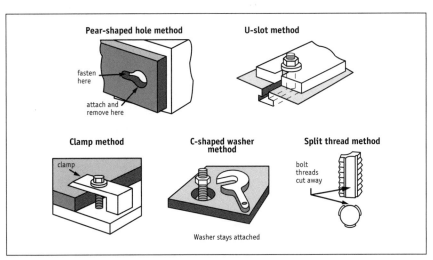

Figure 6-3. One-Turn Functional Clamping Methods

One-Turn Methods

Key Point

As shown in Figure 6-3, *one-turn functional clamping methods* include:

- Pear-shaped hole method
- U-slot method
- Clamp method
- C-shaped washer method
- Split thread method

Let's look at a few examples.

Example

In the *pear-shaped hole method*, bolt holes are made into pear-shaped holes so that nuts on a lid, die, or other part can be loosened in one turn. Once the nuts are loosened, the part can be moved over by one bolt's width. The part can then be lifted off over the bolts without removing the bolts or nuts.

In the *U-slot method*, a U-shaped slot is cut in the attachment edge of a die. By inserting the head of the bolt into a dovetail groove on the machine bed, then sliding the bolt into the U-slot of the die, the die can be fastened with one turn of the nut.

In the *split thread method,* grooves are cut along the length of a bolt to divide it into three sections. Corresponding grooves are cut into the threads on the inside of the nut. Attachment is done by lining up the ridges of the bolt (where threads remain) with the grooves inside the nut (where the threads have been cut away). The bolt is then slipped all the way into position and tightened by a one-third turn.

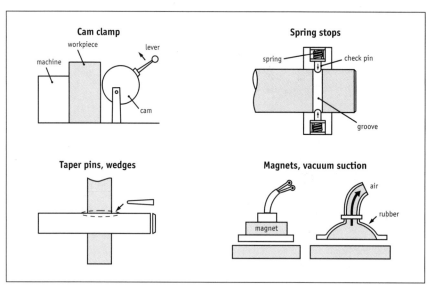

Figure 6-4. One-Motion Functional Clamping Methods

One-Motion Methods

Key Term

Example

Just as the name implies, *one-motion methods* secure an object with a single motion. Figure 6-4 shows several one-motion devices, including:

- Cams and clamps
- Wedges and taper pins
- Spring stops
- Magnets or vacuum suction

Springs, for example, can be used to secure objects in pincer-type or expansion mechanisms. They can also be used as stops inside check pins on the inside diameter of an object. The example in Figure 6-4 shows a spring-loaded check pin on a device for clamping gears onto a shaft.

Magnetism and *vacuum suction* are also very convenient as one-motion methods, especially when the entire surface of the workpiece is to be machined and there is no room for attachment devices. When suction is used, be sure that the surfaces are smooth and no air can leak in.

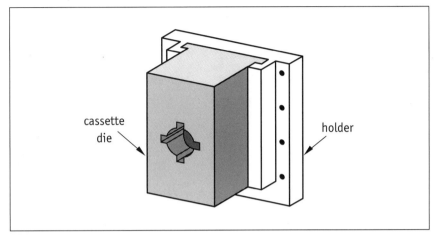

Figure 6-5. An Interlocking Method for Securing Parts

Interlocking Methods

Key Term

Example

Interlocking methods can be simply described as fitting and joining two parts together without the use of a fastener.

For example, in the interlocking method shown in Figure 6-5, not a single bolt is used to clamp the plastic die to the machine. Instead, both the base plate of the die and the machine cradle are provided with tapered surfaces. Attachment and centering precision are achieved by locking those tapered sections together. In other words, this interlocking method is simply a matter of fitting two parts together.

TAKE FIVE

Take five minutes to think about these questions and to write down your answers:

- What one-turn or one-motion methods might be helpful for your setup operations?

- Could parts in your operation be joined with the interlocking method instead of bolts?

Figure 6-6. Making Settings, Not Adjustments

Eliminating Adjustments

Key Point

Recall from Chapter 3 that trial runs and adjustments can account for 50 percent of the time in a traditional setup. *If adjustments can be eliminated, therefore, a lot of machine downtime can be saved.* Bear in mind that when we talk about eliminating adjustments, that's exactly what we mean—*eliminating*, not just reducing.

As Figure 6-6 points out, eliminating trial runs and adjustments is done by making good settings before you ever start up the machine for the new operation. The number of trial runs and adjustments that will need to be made depends on how accurately (or inaccurately) you performed the centering, dimensioning, and condition setting in the earlier steps of setup. To eliminate adjustments, then, we need to refine and standardize how we carry out these earlier tasks.

Key Point

Three practical techniques for eliminating adjustments are:

- Using a numerical scale and making standardized settings
- Making imaginary center lines and imaginary reference planes visible
- Using the Least Common Multiple (LCM) system

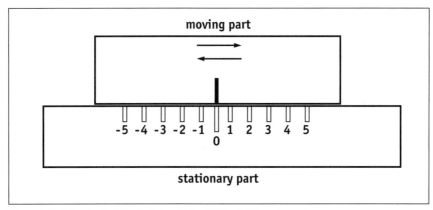

Figure 6-7. A Graduated Scale Helps Make Settings More Accurate

Fixed Numerical Settings

Key Point

Eliminating adjustments requires operators to rely less on intuition and more on constant numerical values for machine settings. The fact is, as good as your intuition may be, it is still not *exactly* the same every time.

Key Term

The first step in doing away with adjustments is to make a *graduated scale* with marks indicating various settings, like the one shown in Figure 6-7. By using a graduated scale, a setting of "5" is more or less the same each time that setting is needed. Although graduations help, however, they will not eliminate adjustments entirely when greater precision is required.

Key Point

Settings made by sight on a scale are usually accurate to within .5 mm (about .02 inch). When greater accuracy is needed, measuring instruments equipped with dial gauges should be used. Dial gauges are accurate to .01 mm (about .0004 inch). Digital numerical control devices are being refined and improved constantly, and you may find you can achieve even greater precision in your workplace.

Key Term

Another numerical setting method uses *gages* or *shims*—spacer blocks with fixed numerical dimensions—to set a distance reliably each time. Gages can be used in various combinations, so that a few different gages can express a wide range of numbers.

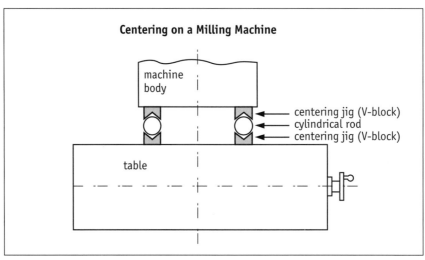

Centering on a Milling Machine

machine body

centering jig (V-block)
cylindrical rod
centering jig (V-block)

table

Figure 6-8. Using Centering Jigs (V-Blocks) to Center the Table Under the Milling Machine

Visible Center Lines and Reference Planes

In a traditional setup operation, center lines and reference planes may not be visible on the machine. This means that the correct position for a tool or workpiece must be found by intuition—or by trial and error. *Making these center lines and reference planes visible is an effective strategy for eliminating these later adjustments.* Several techniques can be helpful.

Key Point

Example

For example, at D Plastics, making a plastic mold involves aligning the center of a milling machine cutter with the center of the work-piece. In the past, the workpiece center line was imaginary, and there was no base reference position because the table of the machine moves back and forth during processing.

In the improved setup, shown in Figure 6-8, two V-blocks were installed on the machine's cutter head parallel to the table's center line to function as centering jigs. Two more V-blocks were installed on the table itself, parallel to this center line. Next, two cylindrical rods were made. By placing the rods in the V-blocks on the table and moving the table to line them up under the V-blocks on the machine, the center of the table is automatically aligned with the center of the cutter. Now when the workpiece is attached to the center of the table, it is automatically aligned with the center of the cutter. Trial cutting is no longer necessary.

TAKE FIVE

Take five minutes to think about these questions and to write down your answers:

• How would calibrations or other fixed numerical settings help eliminate adjustments in your operation?

• How might you make center lines and reference planes visible in your operation?

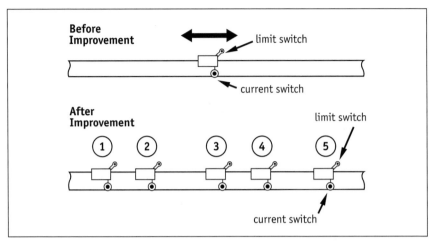

Figure 6-9. Avoiding Adjustments by Installing a Limit Switch at Each Position

Least Common Multiple (LCM) System

Key Term

Many operations performed on one machine have elements in common, where similar things are done but with different dimensions, patterns, or other functions. *The Least Common Multiple (LCM) system* makes these common elements into a mechanism that can handle the different functions needed. During changeover, the mechanism stays in the machine, and only the function changes. In an LCM system, the function is changed by making a quick setting, such as by rotating tools on a spindle or flipping a switch. Thus two basic principles of the LCM system are:

Key Point

1. Leave the mechanism alone and modify only the function.

2. Make settings, not adjustments.

Example

For an example of LCM, look at the "Before Improvement" portion of Figure 6-9. This example involves an operation in which a limit switch controls the end point of machining in the pro- duction of shafts. There are five shaft types, and the single limit switch has to be repositioned at a different point for each type. Every time a different type of shaft is processed, the switch has to be moved, test runs have to be conducted, and adjustments have to be made. In this time-consuming setup process, as many as four readjustments might be needed.

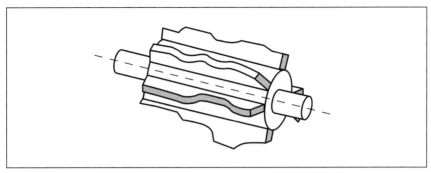

Figure 6-10. A Template That Can Be Changed with a Turn of the Spindle

Now look at the "After Improvement" portion of Figure 6-9.
Notice that an individual limit switch has been permanently
installed at each of the five needed positions. A master current
switch controls the flow of electricity to each individual switch.
This arrangement makes it possible to perform setup changes
simply by flipping the master switch. In other words, setup now
takes about one second.

Example

Another example of LCM involves a lathe that cuts several
different patterns. To make the pattern in the material, the lathe's
cutting tool follows a template; each different pattern has its own
distinct template. Each template is a separate part that has to be
attached and detached from the machine during changeover.

Using the principles of LCM, several different templates are now
brought together in a single mechanism. As Figure 6-10 shows,
the templates are arranged on a spindle that stays in the machine
during changeover. The only change needed is an easy turn of
the spindle to set up the right template for the next job. This
improvement idea saves a lot of setup time and avoids problems
with lost templates and attachment parts.

TAKE FIVE

Take five minutes to think about this question and to write
down your answer:

• How might you apply the Least Common Multiple (LCM)
  system in your equipment changeovers?

Figure 6-11.

Mechanization

Key Point

Mechanization should only be considered after every attempt has been made to streamline setups using the techniques we have already discussed. There are two reasons for this. First, while the general techniques we have discussed can reduce setup times from, say, two hours to three minutes, mechanization will only cut this time by another minute or so.

Key Point

A second reason to avoid jumping straight into mechanization is the fact that *mechanizing an inefficient operation may result in time reductions, but it will not really make the process better* (see Figure 6-11). It is much more effective to mechanize setups that have already been streamlined as much as possible. In short, use mechanization for fine tuning, not for dramatic reduction.

Mechanization is essential for moving large press dies, die-casting dies, and plastic molds. Practical techniques include:

Key Point

- Using forklifts for insertion in machines

- Moving heavy dies on bolsters

- Tightening and loosening dies by remote control

- Using electric drives for shut height adjustments

- Using the energy from presses to move dies

Remember: these techniques should only be considered after you have already streamlined a setup to the three-minute range.

In Conclusion

SUMMARY

The third and final stage of SMED is *Streamlining All Aspects of the Setup Operation*. In this stage, all remaining internal and external setup operations are improved by looking at each operation's function one more time, making each as efficient as possible.

Practical techniques for Stage 3 improvements can be divided into external setup improvements and internal setup improvements. External setup improvements include streamlining storage and transport of parts and tools so that these items are well-organized and ready for the next operation.

Improvement of internal setup operations can be made through four practical techniques. First, parallel operations can be used—dividing the setup operations between two people, one at each end of the machine. The most important issue in conducting parallel operations is safety.

A second method is the use of functional clamps. A functional clamp is an attachment device that holds objects in place with minimal effort and that can be tightened and loosened quickly. Functional clamping systems include one-turn, one-motion, and interlocking methods.

Third, recall that trial runs and adjustments account for up to 50 percent of traditional setup time. By eliminating adjustments, then, setup time can be reduced dramatically. Three practical techniques for eliminating adjustments are fixing numerical settings, making imaginary center lines and reference planes visible, and using the Least Common Multiple (LCM) system.

Finally, mechanization of certain processes should be considered only after every attempt has been made to streamline setups using the other techniques discussed in this chapter. Mechanization should be used for fine tuning, not for dramatic reduction.

REFLECTIONS

Now that you have completed this chapter, take five minutes to think about these questions and to write down your answers:

• What did you learn from reading this chapter that stands out as particularly useful or interesting?

• Do you have any questions about the topics presented in this chapter? If so, what are they?

• What information do you still need to fully understand the ideas presented in this chapter?

• How can you get this information?

Chapter 7

Reflections and Conclusions

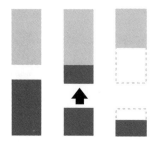

Reflecting on What You've Learned

Key Point

An important part of learning is reflecting on what you've learned. Without this step, learning can't take place effectively. That's why we've asked you at the end of each chapter to reflect on what you've learned. And now that you've reached the end of the book, we'd like to ask you to reflect on what you've learned from the book as a whole.

TAKE TEN

Take ten minutes to think about these questions and to write down your answers:

- What did you learn from reading this book that stands out as particularly useful or interesting?

- Do you have any questions about SMED? If so, what are they?

- What ideas, tools, and techniques have you learned that will be most useful in your own work? How will they be useful?

- What ideas, tools, and techniques have you learned that will be least useful in your work? Why won't they be useful?

Applying What You've Learned

Possible Ways to Apply SMED

The way you decide to apply what you've learned will, of course, depend on your individual situation. If your company is launching a full-scale SMED implementation program, you should have ample opportunity to apply what you've learned right away. In this case, you may be included on a team of people who are responsible for implementing SMED in a certain work area. Or you may have implementation time structured into your work day and may be responsible for reporting the results of your activities on a regular basis.

On the other end of the spectrum, your company may have no immediate plans to implement SMED. In this case, the extent to which you can implement what you've learned will depend on how much control you have over your own schedule, work flow, and work area.

Your Personal Action Plan

Key Point

Whatever your situation, we suggest you create a personal action plan for how you will begin applying the information you have learned from this book. You might start by referring to your own notes about the techniques and tools you think will be most useful to you, then writing down answers to the following questions:

- What SMED techniques can I implement right now that will make my job easier, better, and more efficient?

- How can I involve my coworkers in the implementation of what I've learned?

When you've answered these questions, we suggest that you commit to completing the things you've written down within a certain time, and then make a new plan at the end of that time.

Key Point

It's often good to start with something small that you can comfortably finish in the time you've allowed yourself. If the project is too ambitious or time-consuming you can easily get discouraged and give up.

Opportunities for Further Learning

Here are some ways to learn more about SMED:

- Find other books or videos on this subject. Several are listed on the next page.

- If your company is already implementing SMED, visit other departments or areas to see how they are using SMED techniques and tools.

- Find out how other companies have implemented SMED.

Conclusions

SMED is more than a series of techniques. It is a fundamental approach to improvement. We hope this book has given you a taste of how and why this method can be helpful and effective for you in your work. Productivity Press welcomes your stories about how you apply SMED in your own workplace.

Other Resources Related to SMED

The following resources will provide you with additional education related to shortening changeover time. Each resource is available from Productivity Press.

S. Shingo, *A Revolution in Manufacturing: The SMED System* (Productivity Press, 1985)—This is the sourcebook for *Quick Changeover for Operators*. It includes the story of how SMED was developed, basic principles and reasoning behind SMED, and many case studies and examples of the use of these methods in various industries.

S. Shingo, *Quick Changeover for Operators Learning Package* (Productivity Press, 1996)—This Learning Package set is designed to help you lead an employee learning group in your company using *Quick Changeover for Operators* as the reading material. Each package includes the sourcebook *A Revolution in Manufacturing: The SMED System*, a *Leader's Guide*, overheads, slides, and five copies of *Quick Changeover for Operators*.

The SMED System—A video program that shows how Shingo's SMED system works to improve setup time. The program covers the theory and conceptual stages of SMED as well as practical shopfloor applications.

The Winner's Circle—An introductory video that uses the teamwork and speed of an Indianapolis 500 pit crew to illustrate the principles of quick changeover on the shop floor. The program shows how setup on an 800-ton press was reduced from 22 hours to 10 minutes.

K. Sekine and K. Arai, *Kaizen for Quick Changeover* (Productivity Press, 1992)—This book for advanced SMED practitioners shows how to streamline the setup process even further to reduce downtime. Includes case studies from 9 companies.

H. Hirano, *5S for Operators: 5 Pillars of the Visual Workplace* (Productivity Press, 1996)—This Shopfloor Series book outlines five key principles line workers can use to create a clean, visually organized workplace that is easy to work in. Contains numerous tools, illustrated examples, and how-to steps, as well as discussion questions and other learning features.

M. Greif, *The Visual Factory: Building Participation Through Shared Information* (Productivity Press, 1991)—This book shows how visual management techniques can provide "just-in-time" information to support teamwork and employee participation on the factory floor.

Nikkan Kogyo Shimbun (ed.), *Visual Control Systems* (Productivity Press, 1995)—This book presents articles and case studies describing how visual control systems have been implemented in several different companies.

About the Authors

Shigeo Shingo

Shigeo Shingo was born January 8, 1909 in Saga City, Japan. His career spanned over 50 years in factory improvement methodology. He is considered a cofounder (with Taiichi Ohno) of Toyota Motor Company's just-in-time production system.

From 1976 until his death in 1990, Dr. Shingo consulted and lectured widely, inspiring senior managers and factory workers alike throughout Europe and the United States. He wrote nearly 20 books, many of which have been published in English by Productivity Press. In 1988 he was awarded honorary Doctor of Management degrees by Utah State University and by the Université de Toulouse in France. In that year he designated Utah State University to award the annual "Shingo Prizes for Manufacturing Excellence" to North American businesses, students, and faculty.

About the Productivity Press Development Team

Since 1981, Productivity Press has been finding and publishing the world's best methods for achieving manufacturing excellence. At the core of this effort is a team of dedicated editors and writers who work tirelessly to deliver to our customers the most valuable information available on continuous improvement. Their various backgrounds—art history, English literature, graphic design, instructional design, law, library science, psychology, philosophy, and publishing—provide a breadth of knowledge and interests that informs all their work. Inspiring results is their purpose. They love beautiful books and strive to create designs that please as well as ease our readers' use of our books. They read endlessly to keep abreast of new terminology and changes in both the manufacturing and publishing industries. They learn from our customers' experiences in order to shape our books and off-the-shelf products into effective tools that serve our customers' learning needs.

LEARNING PACKAGE

The Learning Package is designed to give your team leaders everything they need to facilitate study groups on *Quick Changeover for Operators*. Shopfloor workers participate through a series of discussion and application sessions to practice using the tools and techniques they've learned from the book.

The Learning Package:

- Provides the foundation for launching a full-scale implementation process
- Provides immediate practical skills for participants
- Offers a flexible course design you can adapt to your unique requirements
- Encourages workers to become actively involved in their own learning process

Included In Your Learning Package:

- Five copies of *Quick Changeover for Operators*
- One copy of *A Revolution in Manufacturing: The SMED System*
- One 8-1/2" x 11" Leader's Guide
- A set of overhead transparencies that summarize major points
- A set of slides with case study examples

Quick Changeover Learning Package
The Productivity Press Development Team
ISBN 1-56327-126-5
Item # QCOLP-B271

About the Shopfloor Series

Put powerful and proven improvement tools in the hands of your entire workforce!

Progressive shopfloor improvement techniques are imperative for manufacturers who want to stay competitive and to achieve world class excellence. And it's the comprehensive education of all shopfloor workers that ensures full participation and success when implementing new programs. The Shopfloor Series books make practical information accessible to everyone by presenting major concepts and tools in simple, clear language and at a reading level that has been adjusted for operators by skilled instructional designers. One main idea is presented every two to four pages so that the book can be picked up and put down easily. Each chapter begins with an overview and ends with a summary section. Helpful illustrations are used throughout.

Other books in the Shopfloor Series include:

QUICK CHANGEOVER FOR OPERATORS
The SMED System
The Productivity Press Development Team
ISBN 1-56327-125-7 / incl. application questions / 93 pages
Item # QCOOP-B271 / $25.00

5S FOR OPERATORS
5 Pillars of the Visual Workplace
The Productivity Press Development Team
ISBN 1-56327-123-0 / incl. application questions / 133 pages
Item # 5SOP-B271 / $25.00

MISTAKE-PROOFING FOR OPERATORS
The Productivity Press Development Team
ISBN 1-56327-127-3 / 93 pages
Item # ZQCOP-B271 / $25.00

FOCUSED EQUIPMENT IMPROVEMENT
For TPM Teams
Japan Institute of Plant Maintenance
ISBN 1-56327-081-1 / 138 pages
Order FEIOP-B271 / $25.00

TPM FOR SUPERVISORS
The Productivity Press Development Team
ISBN 1-56327-161-3 / 96 pages
Item # TPMSUP-B271 / $25.00

TPM TEAM GUIDE
Kunio Shirose
ISBN 1-56327-079-X / 175 pages
Item # TGUIDE-B271 / $25.00

TPM FOR EVERY OPERATOR
Japan Institute of Plant Maintenance
ISBN 1-56327-080-3 / 136 pages
Item # TPMEO-B271 / $25.00

AUTONOMOUS MAINTENANCE
Japan Institute of Plant Maintenance
ISBN 1-56327-082-X / 138 pages
Order AUTMOP-B271 / $25.00

JUST-IN-TIME FOR OPERATORS
The Productivity Press Development Team
ISBN 1-56327-133-8 / 96 pages
Order JITOP-B271 / $25.00

TO ORDER: Phone toll-free **1-800-394-6868** (outside the U.S., **503-235-0600**), fax toll-free **1-800-394-6286** (outside the U.S. 503-235-0909), e-mail **service@productivityinc.com**, or mail to Productivity, Inc., Dept. BK, P.O. Box 13390, Portland, OR 97213-0390. Send check or charge to your credit card (American Express, Visa, MasterCard accepted). For U.S. orders add $5 shipping for first book, $2 each additional for UPS surface delivery; international customers must call for a quote. We offer attractive quantity discounts for bulk purchases of individual titles; call for more information.

See the Productivity, Inc. online catalog at http://www.productivitypress.com